I0753535

FINISHING LINE PRESS
www.finishinglinepress.com

Black Swan

poems by

Kathleen Shaw

illustrated by

Sherry Ward

Finishing Line Press
Georgetown, Kentucky

Black Swan

For Paul

Copyright © 2026 by Kathleen Shaw
ISBN 979-8-89990-415-8 First Edition
All rights reserved under International and Pan-American Copyright Conventions. No part of this book may be reproduced in any manner whatsoever without written permission from the publisher, except in the case of brief quotations embodied in critical articles and reviews.

Publisher: Leah Huete de Maines

Editor: Christen Kincaid

Cover Art: "Black Swan," collage by Sherry Ward

Inside Art: "Melange" and "Closeline," collages by Sherry Ward

Author Photo: Katelynn Shaw

Cover Design: Elizabeth Maines McCleavy

Order online: www.finishinglinepress.com
also available on amazon.com

Author inquiries and mail orders:
Finishing Line Press
PO Box 1626
Georgetown, Kentucky 40324
USA

Contents

Even in Kyoto,
hearing the cuckoo's cry,
I long for Kyoto.
—Matsuo Basho

Black Swan

I remember when you were a teenager
your strong tan hands on the wheel,
speeding down hills, laughing as I screamed
helpless in the passenger seat.

You loved scaring me like you did
when you were seven, riding an escalator
backward, not holding on, hands at your sides,
taunting me, helpless, ten steps below.

I couldn't reach you. The higher I climbed,
the higher you stepped, looking down at me,
arms at your sides, proving that fear is funny,
you were tough, you were above it.

I see a diving board and the five-year-old
I sent out on it, hands shaking, goosebumps
on gleaming arms. You looked down at the deep
water and ran back to me and a warm towel.

Ten years later, panic dragged you down
into water so murky I couldn't find you, couldn't
reach you, couldn't save you. Only you could save
yourself from some unfathomable Black Swan Event.

Snakes

Don't drink from the faucet
Nana used to say. Use a glass.
A snake might slink out and sting you.

Did she really think snakes slithered
out of faucets? Maybe Nana used to live
on a farm where snake intrusions transpire.

Or maybe snakes could slink to cities
and slide out when Dad was shaving
or my sister was brushing her teeth.

Why would snakes just come when I
was drinking? Would they lurk in the pipe
stealthily waiting for me?

Or did Nana just think that drinking
from the faucet was bad manners that made
me look like a thirsty backwoodsman?

I had so many questions about secrets
and dangers, but time, like a snake, slips away,
and unspoken answers slide down the drain.

Picnics

Summer Sundays, long picnics
with grandparents. In the woods,
I'd find a path, or make a path where
big rocks were chairs and bare spots
were living room, dining room,
kitchen. Or stage, platform, audience.
Sometimes France, beach, mountains.
Then, when hungry, brisk walk back
to grandparents' white hair in sunlight,
kids playing tag, potato salad in a big red
bowl, table manners, splintered
bench. Picnics, grandparents, potato salad,
mountains are evanescent, but
the two worlds I lived in, I live in still.

Sounds of Shisler Street

In sweltering rowhouses, round
whirring window fans surveyed
the sidewalk with giant eyes.

Every afternoon, the Good
Humor man yelled at kids
who didn't order loud enough.

Down the block, a lonely child
practiced Clare de Lune
on an out-of-tune piano.

Neighbors always laughed
when Mrs. Reilly used rusty
scissors to cut her tiny lawn.

In the evening, ladies on metal
gliders paused to listen
to juicy family squabbles.

Why did they all want to trade Shisler
Street for suburbia, where the major
sound was purring Chryslers?

Answers

One December night, when I was
six or seven, while walking
down the street with my mother,
I asked something I'd been wondering about:
"Why are so many songs about love?"
Without another step, without the slightest
breath, without a glance down at me, she said,
"Because love makes the world go round."

I looked up at stars piercing the cold sky.
I already knew from things said in school that,
hard as it was to believe, we were spinning
through space at that moment. People had
always spun through space, without reason
or explanation. Now, after asking one question,
things on this dizzy spinning place were not
as hard to understand as I thought. With that,
I squeezed my mother's hand even tighter
and we continued walking on the starlit sidewalk.

Thomas Whitaker

A Prose Poem: Nana's Story

Uncle Will, your grandfather's brother, came to live with us after he lost his job at the insurance company, and then he lost his house on Catawissa Street. Your grandfather took care of Will's money and gave him just enough each night to buy one beer. He was quiet and didn't cause any trouble, except for just one time when we all went to Lakeside.

It was the Fourth of July when we all went to Lakeside Amusement Park, about ten miles outside town. When it closed, we looked and looked, but we couldn't find Uncle Will, so we had to drive home without him.

Uncle Will knew his way home because he'd often taken his son Tommy to Lakeside when he was little. Will's wife Mary died in childbirth, so Will raised the boy on his own on Catawissa Street. When Will was at work, little Tommy stayed with the lady next door. She had six kids, so she said one more wouldn't make much difference.

Tommy grew up tall and handsome with straight black hair. He was president of his high school class, but right after graduation he got drafted. He became a Master Sergeant and then he got killed at Iwo Jima.

About six months after Tommy died, Uncle Will lost his job at the insurance company and his house on Catawissa Street and came to live with us. Kitty and her three kids were staying with us then, so we couldn't give Uncle Will his own room. He slept on a cot in the dining room. He didn't say much, but he always did the vacuuming for me.

So, getting back to that Fourth of July at Lakeside. Will finally came home the next morning. He'd gone to a bar where some men treated him to a lot more than just one beer. Then he walked all the way home because he didn't want to call in the middle of the night and wake up your grandfather.

He looked terrible after walking ten miles, but he still helped me vacuum that day.

Numbers: 1965

Castor Avenue was Jewish then
delis, yarmulkes,
old bearded men, two by two
arguing in Yiddish,
bearing wrinkled gray suits
and soiled white shirts
to the cleaners where I worked
part-time in my green
Catholic school uniform.

Wives in faded housedresses
bore pin-striped pants and cigar
studded vests, and sometimes
forearms tattooed with black numbers
would slide heavy woolen overcoats
across the Formica counter, but
those numbers meant no more
to me then, than the tiny black numbers
on tags I pinned to their garments.

To Colleen: A Pantoum

The summer before you moved away,
One day it reached a hundred and one.
And we sold Kool-Aid at the bus stop.
It was too far to walk to the pool.

One day it reached a hundred and one.
My knees were covered with scabs.
It was too far to walk to the pool.
We were always avoiding your brothers.

My knees were covered with scabs.
And we ate Fritos on your back porch.
We were always avoiding your brothers,
And we made up our own language.

We ate Fritos on your back porch.
Once we found a dead cat,
And we made up our own language.
We played baseball till the streetlights came on.

Once we found a dead cat.
We played baseball till the streetlights came on
And your mother hid her beer in a drawer
The summer you moved away.

Ode to Corsages

Fifty years ago, you were blossom badges
for those not allowed to earn honorable
mention any other way: dowagers who
got orchids for their faux furs by
staking out the background when flashbulbs
focused on their husbands. You were red roses
on homecoming queens, not permitted
on trophy teams, but lauded for inheriting
blond curls and heart-shaped faces.

You were the unearned pink chrysanthemums
in see-through plastic shells my father always
placed in the refrigerator for me on Easter Eve
to wear to children's Mass. I was half ashamed
of the corny old lady corsage and ungrateful
for the sentimental sentiment. But after he died,
I steeled myself to open the refrigerator door
and see the empty shelf.

Motherhood 1950

Diapers wave from the clothesline. Fresh
air's good for the baby, so I put her in her
playpen out here. He holds her sometimes,
but doesn't change diapers or give bottles.
I take her out of her playpen when she cries
so she doesn't bother him. I take her
to the park in her carriage sometimes so he
can have a break from her crying. She knows
how to wave now and say Dada. Before the war,
he was different. I waved goodbye to one man
and welcomed home another. He works hard,
so I put red lipstick on and brush my hair
before he comes home, and I clean up the house
and get her dressed up real pretty. When
she grows up, I hope she's pretty so she can
get married and have a happy home
like ours. While he's taking his nap, I like to sit
in the backyard and watch the diapers wave
goodbye from the clothesline.

Motherhood 1970

I never got to be June Cleaver
wearing pearls while dusting
and serving homemade cookies
to children with clean cheeks.

Instead, I wore holey jeans
and dragged my baby to protests
where they spoke about a jungle war
and no one shared recipes.

I was raised in a square house
where silent silverware sat
in soldierly rows and laundry
saluted from clotheslines.

The rules for laundry back then
were shirts upside down, socks
right side up, and sheets
with exactly three clothespins.

Then one day the rules blew away.

So I carved a new type of home
where silverware didn't match,
pearls didn't matter, and babies
could crawl on the splintered floor.

Motherhood: 1990

She had it all: data entry in the city,
forty minutes to the suburbs,
pizza on the passenger seat, homework
for three, stories she couldn't sell to little
girls who wanted to believe, bags under
her eyes at forty, husband making three
times as much, his work three times
more important, with three times
the excuses. She had it all, more than
her mothers' mothers who graduated
to Milltown, cigarettes, and bridge
clubs to nowhere. She had it all, more
than hundreds of years of laundry
hanging in the backyard on never-
ending lines. She had it all—what they
dreamed of and more, a dishwasher,
her own car, retirement in 25 years.
Everybody told her she had it all.

Cello

I loved my cello: her burnished
burgundy, curved wooden body, and her
graceful long neck. Every Monday,
Wednesday and Friday in seventh and
eighth grades, I lovingly lugged her to
orchestra practice where we sat across
from the screechy violins.

One night I set her up in the corner
to impress Billy Smith before the eighth
grade dance. She made our living room
look like a musician's mansion.

Out on the street he told the stupid
joke I'd heard a hundred times before:
How do you put that big violin under
your chin? I pretended to laugh.

In high school, I traded in my cello
for cheer-leading pompoms, notes passed
in class, and awkward proms. But even today,
fifty years later, I remember the songs she
sang and the way her bow felt in my hand.

Mélange

She built a nest from shreds:
sliver of straw from far away,
feather from a crow she never met,
cigarette wrapper cellophane,
a partial note someone wrote,
green grass, brown leaves, red yarn,
gray fur from an anonymous cat
to create the nest on my window ledge.

I'm like that scavenger robin
who flew away in a wink of movement.
I've gathered one wrinkled watercolor
from a neighbor's trash, a tarnished mirror
from I can't remember where,
a piano stool from the side of the road,
a rickety rocker where I secretly sit
to admire my counterpart's artwork.

Ode to Gliders

1950s turquoise totems,
escape providers on countless
porches, not grandmotherly
like rockers, more kinetic
than lawn chairs, gliding
hypnotically, going nowhere
on cricket-studded summer nights.

Where did you end up?
Rusting silently in far-off
dumps, next to train sets
and Spam cans, as obsolete
as the clothes we wore
and the things we used to believe.

Ode to the Laundromat

You're an all-night confessional
where the bedraggled and the temporarily
inconvenienced have venials and mortals
washed away in the incoming Tide.
Your Magtags welcome regulars
and newcomers, who, like everyone,
crave a fresh start, a cathartic cleansing
of the soot and spills all fabrics are heir to.
Kids in stained t-shirts worship at the candy
machine and almighty TV. Bachelors stretch out
on gray leatherette couches, as hard and
unforgiving as wooden pews. Babies'
weeping and gnashing of tiny teeth
are drowned out in the mechanical din. Here,
all clothes, sheets, and towels are equal.
All plunge into the same Jordan,
and go through the same agitation cycle,
the same rinse and spin, the same hot dryer.
Then emerge, fragrant and immaculate,
only to be returned once again
to the soiled world outside.

Cemetery Express

The train whistles
its nightly dirge passing
through sleepy neighborhoods.
Nobody tells new passengers
how fast the trip will go,
how fields, horses, houses
whiz by while they're not looking
out the window, thinking
about what happened
five stops back, or spilling
coffee on their laps. The final
destination pulls up. Passengers
say to the empty compartment
air, "Are we there already?
It went too fast." But only silence
answers, and the whistle
no one can ignore.

Glimmer

My walls are painted Glimmer
from the book of many colors
right beside Frosted Fern, Soft Sage,
and Moonstone. Glimmer's a mixture
of Sanctuary White, Bedrock Gray,
and Leapfrog Green. But it's just
a touch, a flicker, a gleam, a ray.
Sometimes a glimmer is all you need
when there's nothing to hold onto,
when he's so far away, out of reach.
I hold onto a glimmer of hope,
a sanctuary, a bedrock, a leap
of faith, when things are gray
and spring's so far away.

ACKNOWLEDGMENTS

I am grateful to the following journals for publishing these poems:

Anthology, "One Summer" (in an earlier version).

Derail, "Motherhood 1970"

Philadelphia Stories, "Little Painting in Yellow," "Melange," and "Ode to Gliders"

Schuylkill Valley Journal, "Black Swan," "Cemetery Express," and "Numbers"

Thank you to my teachers and fellow students at the Creative Writing Program at Rosement College, especially J.C. Todd, who fostered my love for poetry.

My deep appreciation goes to the Montgomery County Poet Laureate Program, instituted by Joanne Leva, whose encouragement has been invaluable, my friend Sherry Ward, whose artwork graces the pages of my book, my granddaughter Katelynn Shaw who took my photos, and my niece Karen Brockenbrough for locating the photo for my prose poem.

Thanks to my daughter and fellow writer, Danielle Shaw, who helped me on countless days in countless ways to put my first book of poems together.

Finally, thank you to Finishing Line Press editors Mimi David and Christen Kincaid for their patience and support.

Kathleen Shaw is a poet, volunteer tutor, former English teacher, amateur watercolor artist, and lover of travel, having visited many European countries with her husband Paul. In many ways, she is a contradiction. She is at heart an introvert who has morphed into an extrovert during her long life. Kathleen was born in a small town where her father worked as a coal miner. Then the family moved to Philadelphia when she was five years old. Her love of poetry awakened when she was the editor of her high school literary magazine. Then, after attending Temple University for two years, she graduated from West Chester University. Later, she taught high school English and then community college after receiving her MA. Subsequently, she earned a second Master of Fine Arts degree from Rosemont College.

Her poetry has appeared in various journals such as *Anthology, Philadelphia Stories,* and *Schuylkill Valley Journal.* Twice she was runner-up in the Montgomery County Poet Laureate competition.

Kathleen is the mother of three children, Danielle, Kevin, and Michael, and four grandchildren, Jordan, Joseph, Alexander, and Katelynn. They, along with her supportive husband of 57 years, Paul, are the loves of her life.

Sherry Ward created the collages for this book. Always a lover of color and pattern, Sherry quilted for many years before taking her first watercolor class thirty years ago. Expanding her studies, she later discovered the pastel medium and fell in love with the brilliance of the color and texture. Today, her interests have expanded and she now includes pallet knife acrylics, mixed media, and collage.

She is a signature member of the Philadelphia Watercolor Society, the Philadelphia Pastel Society, and the Perkiomen Valley Art Center. She enjoys exhibiting her work in local and national shows, taking weekly classes, participating in varied workshops, and selling in local galleries.

To Sherry, living the life of an artist has been very rewarding. She is grateful every day to be able to paint, create, explore, learn, and spend spare time with others who feel the same as she does regarding this amazing and creative process.

www.ingramcontent.com/pod-product-compliance
Lightning Source LLC
LaVergne TN
LVHW052358100826
845147LV00013B/870

* 9 7 9 8 8 9 9 9 0 4 1 5 8 *